HOW TO CHANGE THE WORLD

WORLD

**Surprising Secrets
of Great Scientists**

Isabel Thomas

Illustrated by Esme Lonsdale

D0314118

04075

Contents

Get Ready to Change the World

Have you ever dreamed about changing the world? What do you think you'd need to do?

Think again! You're about to discover what *really* helped great scientists to change the world. Who knew the history of science was paved with:

Showmanship

Fossilized dung

Perspiration

Chocolate bars

Germ soup

Thousands of beetles

Falling apples

Embarrassing mistakes

Accidental explosions

Standing on the shoulders of giants

World-changing science is often the work of many people over many years. The world's best-known scientists were good at improving on previous ideas and discoveries. In turn, their ideas and inventions inspired other scientists. Isaac Newton (page 28) described this as 'standing on the shoulders of giants'.

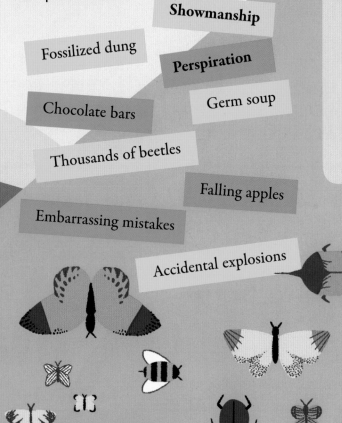

Some scientists had ideas that changed the way we *see* the world. Others made discoveries that changed the way we *live* in the world.

Discover the secrets of their success … and learn how you can change the world too!

Avoid Being
Boiled Alive

Abu Ali al-Hassan Ibn al-Haytham (known as Alhazen) was born in Iraq in 965. He is often described as 'the father of modern **optics**'.

The scientist:
Alhazen

The problem

Alhazen was working in Iraq in the early 1000s when he heard about a problem in Egypt. Every year the River Nile flooded, often destroying crops and causing **famine**. Alhazen loved science and engineering so he offered to solve the problem by building a dam.

The mistake

Unfortunately, Alhazen had never seen the Nile before – in those days there was no Internet. There weren't even cameras! When Alhazen arrived in Egypt, he realized that it would be impossible to build the dam. How could he admit this to the ruler, Al-Hakim, who was said to boil people alive if they annoyed him?

A dam was finally built across the Nile more than 900 years later, in the 1960s. It was built using machinery that wasn't invented in Alhazen's day.

Look up at the sky. Can you work out where Earth's **atmosphere** ends and space begins? Without modern instruments, Alhazen worked out that the atmosphere was around 100 kilometres high.

The way out

Alhazen hatched a plan. He pretended to have lost his mind and was put under house arrest. This gave him lots of time to study science – especially the science of light and sight.

Alhazen investigated everything about light, from shadows and rainbows to the science of sunsets. He bounced light off mirrors and bent it with lenses. He invented the world's first pinhole camera. Most importantly, he backed up his ideas with careful experiments.

Working out HOW we see the world

Alhazen famously found out how we see. When he started his research, most people thought that beams of light travelled out of their eyes and shone on objects so they could see them. Alhazen thought that was nonsense. He carried out experiments to prove that we see when light enters our eyes.

Inside the science

Alhazen experimented with bulls' eyes by dissecting them. He was the first person to describe the different parts of the eye, and explain how the brain and eyes work together to let us see.

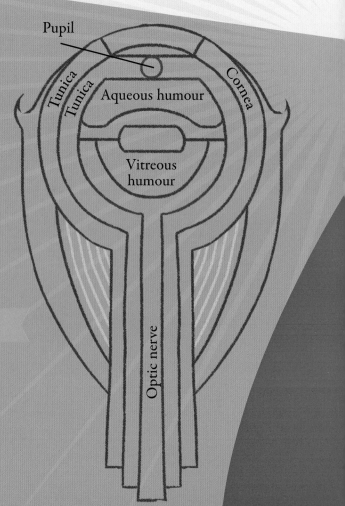

Pupil

Tunica

Tunica

Aqueous humour

Cornea

Vitreous humour

Optic nerve

Top tip for changing the world

Alhazen said the secret to successful science was questioning everything he read and only believing something if he could see it demonstrated with his own eyes.

Alhazen's famous *Book of Optics* influenced scientists for hundreds of years after he wrote it.

A life in science

965 Born in Basra, Iraq

1011 Travels to Egypt to try to dam the Nile. Fails, and pretends to go mad. Imprisoned by the ruler Al-Hakim

1011–21 Studies light and sight during house arrest and writes the *Book of Optics*

1021 Al-Hakim dies and Alhazen is free, but he doesn't stop working

1025–28 Writes a book pointing out all the things another famous thinker – Ptolemy – got wrong

1038 Is the first scientist ever to suggest that Earth is rotating around its axis

1040 Dies in Cairo, having written more than a hundred books and articles on science

What changed?

Other great scientists used Alhazen's experiments and records to build on his work and make famous findings of their own. As well as learning from Alhazen's discoveries about light and sight, they also learnt from the methods he used.

Alhazen was one of the first scientists to conduct experiments to test ideas, and to write everything down in an organized way to produce reliable evidence. This scientific method guided other scientists' work.

Many people consider Alhazen the first real scientist. A Moon crater and asteroid are named in his honour.

 Links within this book

Isaac Newton (page 28) built on Alhazen's discoveries, over 650 years later.

Become an Expert
on Dinosaur Dung!

Mary Anning was a famous fossil hunter! She came from a very poor family in Lyme Regis, Dorset, and spent little time at school. Her father loved collecting fossils and passed on his knowledge to his children. When he died, they made their living from finding and selling fossils. Luckily, the Dorset cliffs were one of the best places in the world to find fossils – and Mary soon became an expert at finding them.

First big discovery

In 1811, when Mary was 12, her brother Joseph spotted an enormous skull protruding from a cliff. Slowly and methodically, Mary dug it out of the rock, along with the rest of the skeleton. The skull was 2 metres long and resembled a crocodile's head. In fact, it was the fossil of a sea creature that had lived 200 million years ago.

Things to do before you're 12:

Climb a tree ✓

Roll down a really big hill ✓

Build a den ✓

Become the world's greatest fossil hunter?

Mary's first big discovery was the Ichthyosaurus ('Fish-lizard'). They could grow more than 9 metres long, with dolphin-like flippers and eyes almost as big as footballs!

Mary spent the rest of her life hunting for amazing fossils in the Dorset cliffs. In the nineteenth century it was very rare for a woman to work in any kind of science.

The best time to find fossils was after a heavy storm, when the cliffs crumbled away to reveal new fossils. It was dangerous work. A landslide in 1833 killed Mary's dog, Tray, and almost killed Mary.

Inside the science

Fossils show us what plants and animals looked like thousands or even millions of years ago. They were formed when a dead plant or animal became buried under layers of rock. We can study them to learn more about how things used to live. For example, Mary found some fossilized dung inside some of the larger creatures she discovered. These helped her to work out what the prehistoric beasts had been eating!

Mary taught herself **geology**, so she could understand the rocks she worked with, and **anatomy**, so she could piece together fossil skeletons and work out what the creatures looked like when they were alive. In modern science we call fossil experts paleontologists.

Mary's famous finds include the first two Plesiosaurus skeletons ever found, and a Pterodactylus. At first, the influential scientist Georges Cuvier didn't believe that Mary's Plesiosaurus could be real. He later admitted that he was mistaken, and Mary became famous!

Mary's sketch of a Plesiosaurus

This painting was one of the first to show what the prehistoric world might have looked like. It is based on fossils that Mary found in Dorset. The painter (geologist Thomas De la Beche) sold copies and gave the money to Mary.

What changed?

Mary's fossils forced people to rethink their ideas about the history of the Earth and living things. Other scientists used them as evidence to support world-changing ideas on **evolution**.

Mary also forced people to rethink their ideas about women in science. She was working at a time when most scientists were wealthy, well-educated men. Despite this, Mary became a respected fossil expert and leading scientists travelled to Dorset to learn from her.

What's next?

Amazing fossils are still being uncovered in Lyme Regis, such as this skeleton of a 195-million-year-old Scelidosaurus.

Links within this book

Thomas Edison (page 14) and Percy Spencer (page 40) were also self-taught scientists. Patricia Bath (page 26) also started her science career when she was still a child.

A life in science

1799 Born in Dorset, UK; Mary and her brother Joseph are the only children of 10 to survive

1800 Struck by lightning but survives

1810 Mary's father dies and her family become even poorer. They keep collecting and selling fossils to bring in money

1811 Uncovers one of the first Ichthyosaurus fossils to be found, which is sold to a collector for £23

1820 Becomes well known after an auction of her fossils

1823 Discovers the first complete Plesiosaurus fossil

1828 Discovers a Pterodactylus fossil

1829 Discovers a Squaloraja fossil

1830 Finds another Plesiosaurus fossil and sells it for £210

1838 Given a pension of £25 per year by scientific societies and the government, for her services to science

1847 Dies in Lyme Regis

1908 Said to have inspired the famous tongue-twister 'She sells seashells on the seashore'

Get Sweaty!

Meet one of the hardest-working scientists ever! Each time Thomas Edison devised a world-changing invention, he didn't stop working. He just got on with the next one!

The scientist:
Thomas Edison

Thomas was born in the United States of America (USA) in 1847. He lost most of his hearing by the time he was 12, but he didn't let this impede him as a scientist.

Thomas made the first steps in many areas that changed the way we live – including recording sound, moving pictures, electric lighting and power.

Recording sound

Thomas invented the world's first machine for recording and replaying sound, by turning sound vibrations into dents on a foil cylinder. This was the first time that anyone had been able to record a speech, song or piece of music and listen to it again!

Thomas Edison's kinetoscope → Television

Moving pictures

Thomas built a machine that showed photographs very quickly in sequence to create moving pictures. This was the start of a new type of entertainment, leading to movies and television.

Lighting up the world

In the 1870s, scientists were on a mission to invent a longer-lasting light bulb. Thomas succeeded by trying out thousands of different materials for his bulb **filament** until he found the right one.

Thomas Edison's light bulb →
Modern electric light

On the grid

Thomas helped to build the world's first power station (see page 16).

Better telegraphs

Telegrams were coded messages sent along wires. At first, only one message could be sent along a wire at a time. Thomas found a way to send four messages through a wire at the same time, in different directions. This was a step towards the development of the telephone.

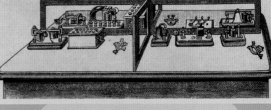

Thomas Edison's quadruplex telegraph → Telephone

Thomas was passionate about inventing. He took naps rather than waste time sleeping at night, and even rushed back to the lab on his wedding day!

Thomas often improved on other people's ideas – that is how he invented his first light bulb. To power bulbs, you need a reliable electricity supply. Thomas developed a system that contained everything needed to produce, supply and use electricity – from a generator at one end to sockets at the other.

Thomas's power station made it safer and cheaper to light homes using electricity. It was the start of a world-changing movement towards electric power. This meant there was increasing demand for the electrical products that Thomas made!

Thomas built the world's first power station, supplying electricity to 85 customers in New York, USA.

Inside the science

Thomas used parallel circuits to supply electricity to lights. Because the light bulbs were connected to different branches of the wire, if one bulb failed, it wouldn't mean that the rest would go out.

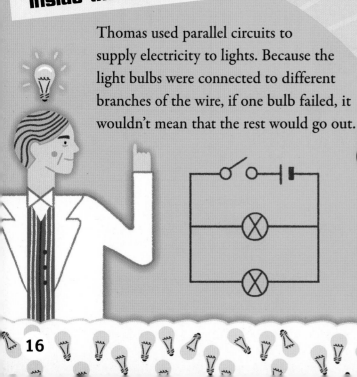

 Snapshot

By the time he died, Thomas had 1093 **patents** for his ideas! This remained a world record for over 70 years.

 Links within this book

Thomas only spent a few months at school and did most of his learning at home. He taught himself by reading books and doing experiments. Mary Anning (page 10) and Percy Spencer (page 40) were also self-taught.

Humphry Davy (1778–1829)
Invented the 'arc lamp', the first lamp to produce light using electricity.

Michael Faraday (1791–1867)
'The father of electricity', who invented the technology to generate electricity in power stations.

James Bowman Lindsay (1799–1862)
Created the first light bulb that could be used without producing smoke or exploding!

Frederick de Moleyns (exact dates unknown)
Won the first patent for an **incandescent** light bulb, using charcoal powder and platinum wires.

Joseph Swan (1828–1914)
Invented the first 'modern' light bulb, which was improved upon by Thomas Edison. The two teamed up to sell their products.

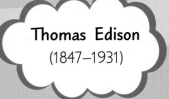

Thomas Edison
(1847–1931)

Werner von Bolton (1868–1912)
Invented the first metal filaments, making bulbs last longer.

William Coolidge (1873–1975)
Invented filaments made out of a metal called tungsten, which made lamps much more efficient.

Live with Your Work

If you want to find out more about chimpanzees, what do you do? Read books? Watch a documentary? Visit a zoo? Jane Goodall had a better plan – she moved to the jungle and lived with chimps for 35 years!

The scientist:
Jane Goodall

Getting close

Jane loved getting close to animals ... really close! When she was 26, Jane had the opportunity to study chimpanzees in Gombe, Tanzania. At the time, scientists knew very little about wild chimps. The Gombe chimps knew very little about humans, and were nervous of Jane. At first she watched them from a distance. The chimps learnt to trust her and allowed her to come closer.

After three years, chimpanzees began to visit Jane in her camp! They treated her like one of their group, saying hello with a touch or a kiss. Jane observed and recorded how the chimps behaved and communicated. She saw them being kind and playful. She also saw them fighting, ganging up on rivals, and even eating other chimps!

Jane quickly realized that chimps had feelings, thoughts and personalities. Other scientists would have identified the chimps by assigning them numbers, but Jane gave them names.

Tool-makers

In November 1960, Jane made an amazing discovery. She watched a chimp called David Greybeard form a twig into the perfect shape for fishing tasty **termites** out of a mound. Chimpanzees could make tools! Later, Jane watched chimps learn tool-making from other chimps.

What changed?

Jane's discoveries changed the world's view of chimpanzees ... and humans! She revealed that humans were not the only **species** that made tools and that chimps and humans were alike in other ways, too.

Scientists still work at the Gombe Stream Research Center that Jane set up, discovering new things about chimp behaviour.

Top tip for changing the world

"... if people don't agree with you, the important thing is to listen to them. But if you've listened to them carefully and you still think that you're right, then you must have the courage of your convictions."

Jane Goodall, 2014

 ### Links within this book

Jane's first job in science was digging up fossils, like Mary Anning (page 10) had done 150 years before.

Start a
Collection

Do you know anyone who's really good at collecting things? Carl Linnaeus built up a collection of 40 000 plants and animals! No wonder he had to invent a new system to organize them all. His system was so efficient that we still use it today.

The problem

Three hundred years ago, explorers were sailing to different parts of the world, helping scientists to discover thousands of new plants and animals. It was exciting, but they had two problems:

1. How to **classify** them in order to understand them.

2. How to name them all.

The scientist

Carl was born in Sweden and worked as a botanist and zoologist. He started his career by training to become a doctor, but what he really loved was studying plants. He managed to fit in plant-collecting expeditions around Lapland and Sweden while he was studying.

Carl came up with a new system for classifying living things. He organized the plants he found into a **hierarchy**. Just like your home address includes a street, village or town, and county, each living thing belonged to a kingdom, phylum, class, order, family, genus and species.

Let's look at the two lowest-ranking of Carl's categories: a genus and a species. A genus is a group of living things that share similar features, for example big cats. A species is an even more specific group of plants or animals that are so similar they can reproduce with each other, for example tigers.

Kingdom: animals
Phylum: chordates
Class: mammals
Order: carnivores
Family: cats
Genus: *Panthera* (big cats)
Species: *tigris* (tiger)

New names

Within the scientific community, most plants had long Latin names that described them in detail. They were easily forgotten, though.

Outside of the scientific community, plants had short names, but they weren't much help to scientists because there were so many different names for the same plant.

English names for 'daisy'

Great ox-eye
Goldens
Moon daisy
Horse gowan
Field daisy
Dun daisy
Butter daisy
Horse daisy
White weed

Carl decided to change the way plants and animals were named, and used their genus and species to describe them. For example, 'daisy' became *Chrysanthemum leucanthemum*.

The first part of the name is the genus.

Great White Shark =
Carcharodon carcharias

The second part is the species.

The two-part names caught on quickly, and everyone started naming living things in the same way. The name was always in Latin, so it could be recognized anywhere in the world.

Carl became famous for his work and people around the globe sent him plants, insects, fish and shells to classify.

Top tip for changing the world

Record your amazing discoveries properly:
"If you do not know the names of things, the knowledge of them is lost too."

Carl Linnaeus, 1751
Philosophia Botanica

Before	After
Chaos! Scientific plant and animal names getting longer and longer.	Plants and animals given simple, two-part names.
Different names used to describe the same plants and animals.	Scientists around the world use the same names for plants and animals.
Grouping of plants and animals based on random things, like where they lived.	Plants and animals grouped according to shared features.
Completely new discoveries meant completely new groups.	It's easier to add new plants and animals to existing groups.

What changed?

Carl's system helped us to understand the natural world, and the relationships between the animals and plants on Earth. Today, every living thing has a scientific name that follows Carl's system. Look out for them on plant labels and medicines.

A million and a half plant and animal species have been classified and named so far – and many scientists have helped. Carl named more than 9000 plants himself.

Carl's collection of plant and animal **specimens** is kept in London. You can visit it in real life or online.

Standing on the shoulders of giants

Aristotle (384–322 BCE) Grouped animals into those with blood and those without blood. His categories now closely relate to our modern classifications of **vertebrates** and **invertebrates**.

Carl Linnaeus
(1707–1778)

Carl Woese (1928–2012) Discovered that – contrary to popular belief – there are actually three types of living things: two types of prokaryote (**bacteria**) and eukaryotes (plants, animals, fungi).

Links within this book

Alhazen (page 6) and Isaac Newton (page 28) also changed the world with their organized approach to science.

Never
Give Up

How many times do you try to solve a problem before giving up? Ten? A hundred? A thousand? It took engineer Nathaniel Wyeth TEN THOUSAND attempts to invent plastic bottles for fizzy drinks.

The scientist:
Nathaniel Wyeth

The 'pop bottle problem'

Fizzy drinks became popular hundreds of years ago, but until the 1970s they were sold in glass bottles. Plastic was cheaper and lighter than glass but fizzy drinks made plastic bottles explode.

Nathaniel saw this as a challenge. He wanted to invent a stronger plastic that was hard to break, stopped the fizz from escaping, and did not **contaminate** drinks.

Glass	Plastic
Transparent	Transparent
Heavy	Lighter
Shatters easily	Harder to break
Strong enough to store fizzy drinks; keeps the fizz in	Swells up and splits when storing fizzy drinks

Inside the science

Nathaniel knew that nylon, a fibre made from oil, gets stronger when it's stretched into a thread. He wanted to make plastic stronger by stretching it in all directions at the same time, like firefighters pulling on a safety net. He splattered melted plastic over the walls of a bottle-shaped mould, weaving it into strong layers.

Top tip for changing the world

"Don't be too quick to accept the way things are being done. Question whether there's a better way."

Nathaniel Wyeth

Breakthrough

Nathaniel worked on his invention for more than five years. He and his team made almost 10 000 bottles by hand.

One day, Nathaniel and his assistant opened their plastic mould and saw something different. Nathaniel said: "This time, at first glance, it looked as if the mould was empty. A closer look revealed something else: a crystal-clear bottle."

Using a more elastic (stretchy) plastic gave Nathaniel the perfect lightweight, transparent and shock-resistant bottle.

Nathaniel's bottles were put into production in the 1970s. His plastic (known as PET) quickly became the standard material for 2-litre soft drink bottles. Today, billions of bottles are produced every year.

Links within this book

Despite the fact that PET is easily recyclable, plastic pollution is still a big problem. Nathaniel is not the only scientist whose invention had unexpected bad consequences, as well as useful ones. Read the story of Alfred Nobel on pages 48–49.

Recycling

Nathaniel didn't know it at the time, but PET is very easy to recycle. Used bottles can be turned into many different things and PET is the world's most recycled plastic.

Start with a Chemistry Set

Patricia Bath was born in New York, USA, in 1942. Her amazing science career started with a gift from her mother – a chemistry set. Patricia was so clever, she finished secondary school in just two and a half years. She went on to become a doctor and inventor who made it her mission to treat and prevent blindness around the world.

The scientist:
Patricia Bath

Patricia worked as an ophthalmologist (eye doctor). She looked for ways to help people who lost their sight because they couldn't pay for eye care. Not only did she operate on people for free, she introduced the idea of 'community ophthalmology', which trained volunteers to spot eye problems in people who wouldn't normally be able to visit a doctor.

The problem

Up to 20 million people around the world are blind due to a condition called cataracts. The lens of one or both eyes turns cloudy, so light can't get in and the patient can't see. There is a cure – cutting into the eye, slicing off the cloudy lens and replacing it with an artificial one. However, in many countries this surgery isn't easily available.

Cataracts are the most common cause of blindness. Most cataracts develop with old age, so as people live longer, the problem will grow.

The solution

Patricia's most famous idea was a tool to make cataracts operations easier and more precise. It uses a **laser** beam to **vaporize** cataracts through a tiny cut in the patient's eye. After the cataract has been zapped, the lens can be removed and replaced.

Patricia's idea was very good, but when she talked to people about it they said it couldn't be done. At the time, lasers were rare. It took Patricia nearly five years to make a working model and prove that her invention made cataract operations more precise.

Patricia's Laserphaco Probe is being used and trialled around the world, and may become the main method of cataract surgery in the future.

Top tip for changing the world

"Do not allow your mind to be imprisoned by majority thinking. Remember that the limits of science are not the limits of imagination."

Patricia Bath

Links within this book

Alhazen (page 6) founded the science of optics. Isaac Newton (page 28) experimented with his own eyes – yuck!

Spend More Time in the Garden

Isaac Newton was the first person to explain how the universe works. He came up with his theory while lounging around in the garden of his family home …

… but Newton's family home wasn't your average family home. It was Woolsthorpe Manor in Lincolnshire, UK. And this is the garden:

Look at this tree. Look really hard. Do any world-changing ideas pop into your head? It inspired Isaac to make one of the greatest scientific discoveries ever.

As Isaac watched an apple fall to the ground, he started thinking about the force that made it fall. Why did it move down, and not up or sideways? He realized that a force called gravity pulls objects down towards the centre of the Earth.

Inside the science

Isaac explained that gravity acts everywhere in the universe, not just on Earth. Gravity holds planets in place as they orbit the Sun; and it holds the Moon in place as it moves around the Earth. Every object in the universe – including you – pulls other objects towards it. Isaac realized that the bigger an object is, the stronger the pull.

What changed?

Isaac published his theories more than 325 years ago, in 1687, but they are still very influential today. Whether someone builds a bridge, kicks a football or launches a space rocket, Isaac's laws mean they can be sure of the outcome.

Scientists also learnt important lessons from Isaac's methods. He carried out experiments to test all his ideas, collecting evidence and writing careful notes.

In *Principia*, Isaac wrote down more than 500 pages of brilliant ideas. His laws explain why everything on Earth moves in the way it does.

Standing on the shoulders of giants

Nicolaus Copernicus (1473–1543) First to suggest that the Earth is not at the centre of the universe and that the Earth moves around the Sun.

Galileo Galilei (1564–1642) Used a telescope to look at space and found things never seen before – things that supported Copernicus's ideas.

Johannes Kepler (1571–1630) Worked out the path that planets take around the Sun.

Isaac Newton (1643–1727)

Emilie du Chatelet (1706–1749) Translated Isaac's famous book, *Principia*, so it could be used by herself and other French scientists.

Albert Einstein (1879–1955) Came up with a new explanation of gravity.

Links within this book

Isaac's discoveries about optics built on the work of Alhazen (page 6).

Put on a Good Show

The scientist:
Guglielmo Marconi

Guglielmo Marconi wasn't the first to invent radio. But he was brilliant at turning big ideas into reality – and getting the world excited about them.

Guglielmo left school with no qualifications but this didn't stop him from winning the world's top science award – the Nobel Prize.

The scientist:
Guglielmo Marconi

The problem

We're surrounded by invisible radio waves, zooming through air, space and even solid objects. They were discovered in the 1880s and scientists soon worked out how to produce as well as detect them. This was very exciting because it allowed people to send signals without using wires.

But there was a problem. As radio signals travelled over long distances, they overlapped and interfered with each other. The receiver at the other end picked up a jumble – or nothing at all.

Eighteen-year-old Guglielmo was fascinated by these radio waves. He began experimenting from his family home and within three years he built equipment that could send radio signals more than two kilometres.

MARCONI FIRST WIRELESS MESSAGE 1895

The solution

In 1896, Guglielmo put on a public demonstration of 'wireless' communication and wowed crowds in London. Today we are used to Wi-Fi, but 120 years ago these invisible signals seemed magical. Guglielmo became known as 'the inventor of wireless' (which annoyed other scientists who'd been working on radio at the same time!).

Guglielmo began working hard to send signals even further: 400 metres, 500 metres, 2500 metres, 5 kilometres, 14 kilometres. Each new distance was a media event. The world was hooked!

Guglielmo set himself a new challenge: to send a radio signal from Europe to North America, across the vast Atlantic Ocean. In 1901, he succeeded. Orders for his equipment flooded in.

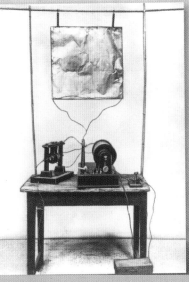

Guglielmo's first radios could only send messages in Morse Code.

Titanic

One of Guglielmo's most famous customers was the company that built the *Titanic*. The ship was fitted with top-of-the-range Marconi equipment. When the ship hit an iceberg and began sinking, the crew sent SOS signals to nearby ships. Guglielmo was celebrated for helping to save the 705 people who were rescued from the icy ocean.

This is the radio room on the *Titanic*. Sending a radio message back to shore would have cost passengers almost £50 in today's money – much more expensive than a text message!

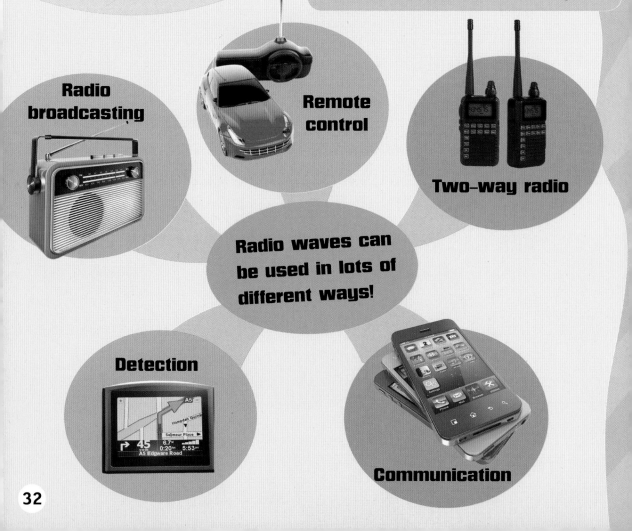

Radio broadcasting

Remote control

Two-way radio

Radio waves can be used in lots of different ways!

Detection

Communication

What changed?

Guglielmo was brilliant at keeping radio – and his name – in the headlines. Each show-stopping demonstration helped him to convince the world that everyone should be communicating by radio. Each success helped him to win support and money for his next big idea.

From Hollywood to the history books

You don't have to do science as a day job to come up with a world-changing idea. Hedy Lamarr was one of the most famous movie stars of the 1940s. She also loved science.

In her spare time, Hedy helped to invent a 'secret communications system' that is now a key part of wireless communication. It stops other people picking up your mobile phone calls by changing frequencies. Every time you use Wi-Fi, Bluetooth or a mobile phone, you have Hedy to thank.

The scientist:
Hedy Lamarr

Standing on the shoulders of giants

Guglielmo was good at developing the ideas of other people, whose breakthroughs helped him at different times.

Heinrich Hertz (1857–1894)
First to produce and detect radio waves. Guglielmo studied his theories.

Nikola Tesla (1856–1943)
The first person to develop practical uses for radio. Just months after Nikola died, Guglielmo's patent was overturned and Nikola was recognized as the real inventor of radio.

> **Guglielmo Marconi**
> (1874–1937)

Reginald Fessenden (1866–1932)
First person to send the sound of his voice via radio, and the first to send speech hundreds of miles across an ocean.

Ambrose Fleming (1849–1945)
Helped Guglielmo to send radio signals across the Atlantic and developed equipment that made it possible to send speech and other sounds.

Edwin Armstrong (1890–1954)
Made radios easier to use and invented FM radio.

Don't Abandon the Old Ideas

In the early 20th century, the world was falling in love with new materials. 'Old-fashioned' cotton was in crisis. Ruth Rogan Benerito helped to save the day by teaching an old fabric new tricks.

The scientist: Ruth Rogan Benerito

Cotton is a natural fibre. It's tough, but comfortable and cool to wear, and can be dyed easily.

The problem

Humans have been making cotton clothes for at least 7000 years. But in the 1950s and 1960s, cotton's popularity was under threat. **Synthetic** fabrics such as nylon and polyester were taking the world by storm. They had useful features like not needing to be ironed.

Cotton had one big problem: it creased really easily and ironing it was hard work. Everyone hates chores, so people were choosing synthetic clothes instead. This was terrible news for the cotton industry. Falling demand meant that cotton farmers would go out of business.

Ruth worked as a chemist for the US Department of Agriculture. Problem-solving was her speciality. Ruth didn't give up on cotton as a fabric. She looked for ways to make it better.

Ruth and her team looked deep inside natural fibres, such as cotton and wood, to understand how they were made up, and how to change their properties. They realized that, instead of treating the outside of the cotton, they needed chemicals that would get inside the fibres and change the way they behaved.

Ruth's team tried out many different treatments before they perfected wrinkle-free cotton. At first, the chemical formaldehyde was used to treat the cotton. This did the job quite well, but was smelly and poisonous to people and animals!

Inside the science

The properties of a material depend on how it's made up inside. The **molecules** in cotton fibres are a bit like the legs of a ladder. Ruth added chemicals that fastened on to the cotton and acted as 'rungs', holding the molecules in place and keeping the fabric smooth.

Cotton fibres

The solution

Ruth's idea meant that manufacturers could make wrinkle-free cotton that you could just 'wash and wear'. This had a huge impact on everyday life. 'Easy-care' cotton is responsible for comfortable, natural clothes that don't take ages to iron – freeing people up to do other things.

Once Ruth's team found out how to attach chemicals to cotton, they could add chemicals that did different jobs – such as making cotton fire-resistant, or less likely to stain.

Ruth registered 55 patents for her brilliant new ideas and discoveries. She also won many awards. Thanks to her dedication to helping cotton move with the times, cotton is still the most used fibre in the world.

Astronaut wearing a suit made of fire-resistant cotton

Ruth's team made sure demand for cotton continued to grow, despite competition from synthetic fibres.

Top tip for changing the world

"No one person discovered it or was responsible for it. But I contributed to new processes of doing it."

Ruth Rogan Benerito

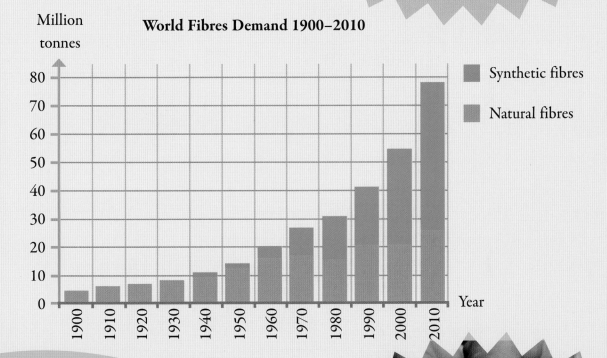

World Fibres Demand 1900–2010

Million tonnes

Synthetic fibres

Natural fibres

Year

What's next?

Biologists are experimenting with ways to grow cotton in different colours, so that it doesn't have to be bleached and dyed.

No Problem?
No Problem!

Sometimes world-changing science is a result of careful planning and experiments. Sometimes it's an accident! Spencer Silver changed the world when he came up with a solution without knowing what the problem was.

The scientist:
Spencer Silver

The solution

Spencer worked at a company called 3M, which made glue. In 1968 he was trying to develop "bigger, stronger, tougher **adhesives**" when he accidentally made a glue that was not very strong and could be used over and over again. Spencer spent years trying to convince his company to find a way to use it. But no one else was interested.

Spencer Silver and Arthur Fry

"I came to be known as
Mr Persistent because
I wouldn't give up."

Spencer Silver

The problem

Fast-forward five years, and Spencer's colleague Arthur Fry had a problem. He sung in a choir and the paper scraps he used to mark pages in his hymn book kept falling out. Arthur had an idea. Perhaps Spencer's not-too-sticky glue could be used on the back of bookmarks.

With a problem to solve, Spencer and Arthur's company let them turn their idea into a real product. It took another five years to design and build machines to make the sticky notes. In 1980, the first Post-it® Notes went on sale. They weren't just bookmarks – they were a whole new way to communicate!

Inside the science

The glue on Post-it® Notes is made up of tiny 'microspheres', with gaps to stop them from sticking too well. A special coating on the back of the notes means the glue sticks permanently to *them,* but does not come off on *other* surfaces. The recipe remains top secret!

What changed?

Once Post-it® Notes were on sale they 'spread like a virus'. When people saw them being used, everyone wanted some. Today more than 4000 types of Post-it® Notes are used around the world. Many other companies in over 150 countries also make 'stickies'.

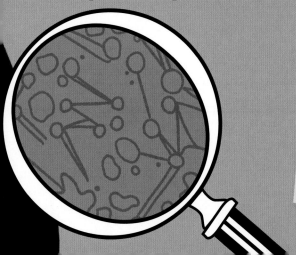

Always
Carry
Chocolate

Percy Spencer was an electronics genius, but his most famous discovery was accidental. His recipe for changing the world included chocolate, popcorn and exploding eggs. The result? Not a 'rocky road' cake, but a cooking revolution.

The scientist:
Percy Spencer

In 1945, Percy was working in his laboratory designing **radar** equipment. He stopped to look at a magnetron – a device that **emits** a special type of wave. Suddenly he noticed a strange feeling. A chocolate bar in his pocket was melting.

Percy decided to investigate. He held a packet of corn kernels next to the magnetron and ... POP! He had made popcorn! His next step was to attempt to concentrate the rays – by creating an 'oven' out of an old kettle. Percy tried cooking an egg in the kettle, but it exploded in his assistant's face.

A magnetron

What is radar?

The waves given out by a magnetron are called microwaves. They are useful for sending signals over long distances. A radar unit sends out bursts of microwaves. When they hit objects, the waves bounce back to the radar unit, which calculates the size and position of the object they bounced off.

Percy discovered that microwaves had another use – they could also cook food, and much more quickly than a normal oven.

Inside the science

Normal ovens work by heating up the air inside the oven, which then heats the food. Microwave ovens work by heating up the water inside food. When the water molecules in food absorb the microwaves, they move around faster and faster, heating up and cooking the food.

Microwave ovens

Percy was highly skilled at turning scientific theories into practice. He began designing a new type of oven that used microwaves. The first 'radarange' was tested in a restaurant in 1946. 'Range' is another word for oven. The ranges were bought by restaurants so they could cook large quantities of food quickly.

This was one of the first microwaves that was made for homes. These early microwaves were marketed as 'dream cookers' and cost thousands of pounds. They didn't catch on until Percy's company introduced a cheaper and smaller version of their radarange in 1967.

Never experiment with microwaves, or touch a microwave without adult supervision. Microwaves don't just cook food – they could cook people too!

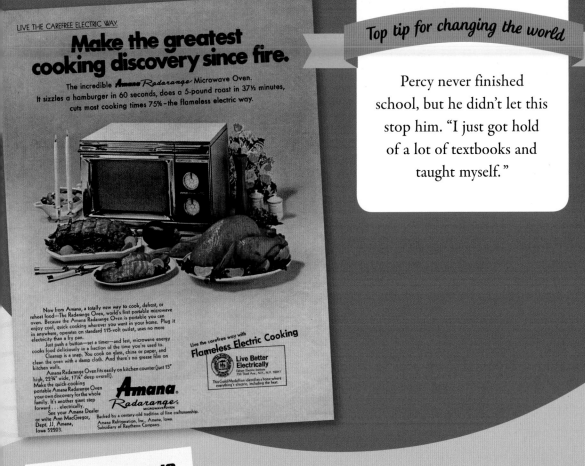
Top tip for changing the world

Percy never finished school, but he didn't let this stop him. "I just got hold of a lot of textbooks and taught myself."

What changed?

Microwaves took a while to win the world over. The first models left food hot, but not very tasty. Companies developed the technology to make smaller, simpler, cheaper microwave ovens. By 1975, more microwaves were being sold in the USA each year than gas ovens. People found they could prepare whole meals in minutes, saving time for other things.

Today, hundreds of millions of microwaves are used in homes all around the world. Microwaves are also important in industry, for heating and drying out products quickly.

Links within this book

Sometimes solving one problem can create a new one. Percy could not have predicted that microwaves would lead to a rise in unhealthy 'ready meals'. Find out about the unpredicted consequences of Nathaniel Wyeth's and Alfred Nobel's discoveries on pages 24 and 48.

Stick to Your Guns

Charles Kao was born in 1933, in China. His world-changing work in laboratories in Harlow, UK, won him the Nobel Prize in Physics in 2009.

Instant messaging, video streaming, social networks and online games rely on a super-fast Internet. They are possible because Charles Kao had a brilliant plan to improve **telecommunications** and didn't listen when everyone said it was unrealistic.

The problem

Today the world is criss-crossed with fibre optic cables which carry information at incredible speeds over land and under oceans. But fifty years ago, telephone messages were sent through copper wires. They could only carry a small amount of information at a time. As more people started to make calls, the world faced a telephone traffic jam.

The solution

In the 1960s, Charles thought of a brand new way to send information around the world. He wanted to use light, which travels much faster than electricity. Light cannot travel through copper, but it can travel through glass. Charles wanted to beam light signals through thin glass tubes.

Everyone said this was crazy. There were too many problems! How could he generate the light? How could he stop the light from escaping and fading? What would happen if the tube bent? But Charles was certain that his idea would work. With careful experiments, he and his team solved these problems one by one.

In 1966, Charles began to tell the world about fibre optics. He said it was like "trying to sell a dream" because he couldn't show anyone a fibre optic network in action – it was just an idea. Eventually, the first fibre optic telephone messages were sent in 1977. Charles went on to rewire the whole planet!

What changed?

Most of the world's long-distance telephone and computer communication cables are now optical. They are changing the way we communicate.

Most short-distance cables (bringing information to our homes) are still copper. As they are replaced with fibre optic cables, communication will keep getting faster. This makes it easier to work, learn and access entertainment from home.

Top tip for changing the world

"In the next 1000 years, I can't think of a better system [than fibre optics]. But don't believe what I say, because I didn't believe what experts said either."

Charles Kao

Each optical fibre is a long glass cylinder as thin as a hair. The fibres are bundled together to make cables. Messages are sent as pulses (flashes) of laser light. Each pulse enters a fibre at one end and travels to the other end by 'bouncing' off the walls of the cylinder. It works because light is always reflected at the same angle that it strikes a surface. If this angle is big enough, no light escapes from the glass fibre. This is called total internal reflection.

Narinder Singh Kapany was the first person to develop the science behind fibre optics. When a teacher told him that it was impossible to bend light, Narinder set out to prove him wrong! He discovered how light is reflected along a glass fibre (see above), and that adding a coating to a fibre made the light travel further.

The scientist:
Narinder Singh Kapany

Other applications

Scientists have also developed short-range uses for fibre optics, including medicine, mechanics and plumbing.

A fibre optic endoscope is an instrument that can look inside a person's body without causing damage, and send images back to a doctor. The same technique can be used to examine a machine, such as a rocket in space, without taking it apart!

 **Snapshot**

Laid end-to-end, the world's optical cables could circle the planet 25 000 times.

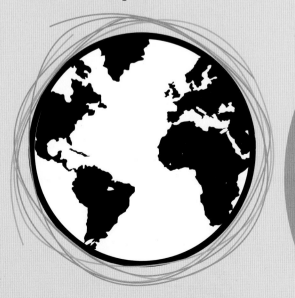

What's next?

Fibre optic cables have been used to build a new Internet called the Grid. Connecting to the Grid could bring us information 10 000 times faster. This could allow us to do amazing things, such as beaming friends into our homes as holograms for **virtual** meet-ups!

Be Careful What You Change

The scientist:
Alfred Nobel

Science has made the world a healthier, more comfortable and better-connected place. It has helped people to produce more food and brought new types of fun and entertainment. But scientific discoveries can have unexpected consequences too, as Alfred Nobel found when he invented dynamite.

The problem

It began when Alfred started experimenting with a new explosive. An Italian chemist had invented nitroglycerin by mixing glycerol (the sweet-tasting liquid in cough syrup) with some nasty acids. It was much more powerful than gunpowder, and exploded far too easily.

Alfred set out to find a way to make nitroglycerin safer to handle – a dangerous job in itself. There were many accidental explosions and one of them even killed Alfred's brother.

Top tip for changing the world

"If I have a thousand ideas and only one turns out to be good, I am satisfied."

Alfred Nobel

In 1866, Alfred discovered that mixing nitrogylcerin with chalky sand turned it into a paste that could be handled more safely. He called this new mixture dynamite. Alfred also invented the detonator and blasting cap to make explosives safe and easy to use.

Dynamite paste could be shaped into rods and pushed into holes in rocks to blast them apart.

The Nobel Prizes

When Alfred died, his **will** contained a surprise. He left most of his fortune to set up an award for scientists and others who have "conferred the greatest benefit on mankind".

The first Nobel Prize was awarded in 1901. Every year there are prizes for the very best achievements in physics, chemistry, medicine, economics, peace and literature.

No one knows exactly why Alfred did this, but it may be because he was shocked that a newspaper had described him as a "**merchant of death**".

What changed?

Alfred's invention made it easier, cheaper and safer to break up rock for building roads, canals and railways. He set up dynamite factories around the world and made a fortune.

However, dynamite – and the more powerful explosives that followed it – had another, deadlier use. They gave humans a weapon that could do massive damage.

Links within this book

Alfred is not the only scientist whose discoveries had good and bad consequences. When Nathaniel Wyeth invented plastic bottles (page 24), he did not realize there would be a huge problem with plastic pollution. When Percy Spencer invented the microwave (page 40), he did not predict that it would lead to a rise in unhealthy eating.

Be a Guinea Pig!

A 'guinea pig' is someone or something that is the subject of an experiment. Although some of the scientists in this book experimented on themselves, you should *never* perform any experiments on yourself.

The scientist:
Barry Marshall

Science is all about careful tests and trials to prove that an idea is right. When the world refused to believe Barry Marshall's theory about a very common and painful illness, he decided to prove it by testing it on himself.

The problem

Stomach ulcers are nasty sores on the stomach wall. If they get really bad, they can make a hole in the stomach lining. Because stomachs are full of acid, this is very painful. In the past, some patients got so ill they had to have parts of their stomachs cut out to stop the pain and bleeding.

The scientist

Barry came across the horrible effects of stomach ulcers when he was training as a doctor. One of his colleagues had found strange bacteria in the stomachs of some patients. Together, they began looking for evidence that linked the strange bacteria to stomach ulcers. They did this alongside their day jobs in medicine.

Barry was convinced that a bacterial infection was causing the stomach ulcers. He shared his theory with other scientists but most thought it was a silly idea. They said that bacteria could never live inside the stomach, with such strong acid sloshing around. Everyone thought that ulcers were caused by stress, or spicy food. Barry needed proof.

The solution

Barry drank a dishful of bacteria from someone suffering from stomach ulcers. Barry became very ill and a **biopsy** proved that the bacteria had set up home in his stomach. Of course, Barry already knew how to cure himself – with a course of **antibiotics**.

What's next?

Barry's nasty bacteria may change from harmful to helpful – he is working on a way to use them to give flu vaccines to patients.

What changed?

Barry's self-experimentation helped him to win support and money for trials to prove that antibiotics could cure stomach ulcers. Barry was able to treat patients who had spent years suffering. Instead of dangerous surgery, he prescribed a simple, cheap cure: two weeks of medicine. The treatment of stomach ulcers was changed forever and Barry's work won him a Nobel Prize in Medicine.

Top tip for changing the world

"The concept of a germ causing ulcers was like saying that the Earth is flat. After that, I realized my paper was going to have difficulty being accepted. You think, 'It's science; it's got to be accepted.' But it's not an absolute given. The idea was too weird."

Barry Marshall

Spread the Word

Science can't change the world if it's kept secret. Some scientists have a knack for explaining their work to the public and inspiring people to become scientists themselves.

Science in your living room

Sir David Attenborough is a naturalist famous for capturing wildlife on camera. His interest in natural history started with a childhood fossil collection, just like Mary Anning (page 10).

Sir David has introduced hundreds of millions of people to almost every habitat on Earth. An estimated 500 million people worldwide watched his TV series *Life On Earth*.

Several species have been named after Sir David, including the plesiosaur *Attenborosaurus conybeari* and the tiny goblin spider *Prethopalpus attenboroughi*. (Find out about naming wildlife on page 20.)

Stellar career

Space scientist Dame Jocelyn Bell Burnell changed the way we see the universe when she discovered a type of star never seen before: a pulsar. After breaking down barriers for women in science, Dame Jocelyn hopes to get more girls into super science careers. (Find out more about amazing female scientists on pages 10, 18, 26 and 34.)

The scientist:
Maggie Aderin-Pocock

Touring the universe

Look out for Maggie Aderin-Pocock describing the wonders of space on television. This British scientist also gives science talks around the world. She has had an exciting science career herself, including designing instruments for the James Webb Space Telescope.

The best Christmas present

Michael Faraday changed the world with his discoveries about electricity. He also changed the way the world sees scientists, by setting up the Royal Institution's Christmas Lectures.

Every year, a crowd of young people can watch a brilliant scientist do spectacular demonstrations. Michael gave the first lectures himself, in 1825. Today you can watch them on TV or online – thanks to electricity!

From pretend madness to self-experimentation, the secret to science success is often unpredictable. But one thing links all the scientists in this book: curiosity. Whether they set out to answer a question, or stumbled across something interesting by accident, these incredible scientists kept on asking questions.

If you are curious, and not afraid to challenge other people's ideas, you have the potential to make a great scientist. You could even change the world.

YOU can change the world!

Glossary

adhesives: sticky substances

anatomy: study of the bodies of humans and other animals

antibiotics: medicine that kills bacteria, or stops them from growing

atmosphere: gases that surround Earth

bacteria: tiny living things that can cause disease

biopsy: small sample of body tissue removed for testing

classify: sort into groups based on shared features

contaminate: make something impure

emits: gives out

evolution: process of living things developing over time

famine: a time when food is very scarce

filament: tiny wire or thread which gives out light when electricity flows through it

geology: study of the Earth and rocks

hierarchy: system of ranking things

incandescent: gives out light when heated

invertebrates: animals without a backbone

laser: device that uses light for drilling or cutting

merchant: someone who sells or trades

molecules: tiny building blocks of a substance

optics: the science of light and sight

patents: official documents that give someone the right to make, use or sell something

perspiration: sweat

radar: system that uses radio waves to detect the location of something

showmanship: the skill of putting on a good show to entertain people

species: group of living things that are similar

specimens: plants, animals, fossils or rocks collected by scientists

synthetic: made by humans; not natural

telecommunications: transferring information using signals

termites: ant-like creatures

vaporize: turn into a gas

vertebrates: animals with a backbone

virtual: generated by technology

will: legal document that states a person's wishes for after their death

Index

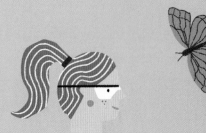

About the Author

I wrote my first non-fiction books when I was at primary school. The main topics were family holidays, school trips and my sisters' strange habits! As a teenager, I studied the science of people and animals at Oxford University. This gave me LOADS of new things to write about. Today, I write books and websites about science for children. I have three young sons who love trying out experiments for me!

I wanted to write this book to tell you about the amazing stories behind scientists' inventions and discoveries, and to show what an adventure science is. Can you imagine being the first person in the world to discover something? Such as my sisters' strangest habits ... I'd tell you, but I've run out of space!

Greg Foot, Series Editor

I've loved science ever since the day I took my papier mâché volcano into school. I filled it with far too much baking powder, vinegar and red food colouring, and WHOOSH! I covered the classroom ceiling in red goo. Now I've got the best job in the world: I present TV shows for the BBC, answer kids' science questions on YouTube, and make huge explosions on stage at festivals!

Working on TreeTops inFact has been great fun. There are so many brilliant books, and guess what ... they're all packed full of awesome facts! What's your favourite?